TO YOUR ROOM!

by

Bil Keane

FAWCETT GOLD MEDAL • NEW YORK

A Fawcett Gold Medal Book
Published by Ballantine Books

Copyright © 1978 The Register & Tribune Syndicate, Inc.
Copyright © 1982 The Register & Tribune Syndicate, Inc.

ISBN 0-449-12610-2

This edition published by arrangement with
The Register & Tribune Syndicate, Inc.

Manufactured in the United States of America

First Fawcett Gold Medal Edition: May 1982
First Ballantine Books Edition: April 1983
Eighth Printing: May 1988

"I can't come out. I'm being punished."

"If I put everything away I'll forget to play with them."

"We ARE in bed!"

"I don't buy the bit about the beanstalk grow-
ing so big overnight."

"Mommy, is this a freckle on my cheek or a measle?"

"I don't WANT to sit on my thumb, Daddy!"

"Why are you brushing its teeth?"

"My mommy and daddy are separated. She's
in the kitchen and he's in the basement."

"I'm gonna say my prayers, Daddy. Is thēre anything you want?"

"Why didn't Cinderella join Women's Lib?"

"History repeated itself. I got another D in it."

"Then the groundhog comes out of his hole
and brings toys for good girls and boys."

"Why don't you tell us to go watch tele-
vision?"

"If you act right now you can get four records
for only $9.98 and a bonus surprise.
Can I have the surprise?"

"Can we stay up till Uncle Bob starts his argument."

"It's addressed to PJ. He's on his first mailing list."

"Jeffy took one for each hand and one for his mouth!"

"Here's another good one, Grandma. Betcha can't answer this one: 'What has four wheels and flies?'"

"Goodness! There's a little boy under all that dirt!"

"Where, Mommy, where?"

"Grandma thanked me for the lovely birthday gift. What did I give her?"

"I found you an ashtray. Mommy can't STAND cigarette smoke!"

"That's an 'O.' To make a 'Q' you just put a
handle on it."

"Freeze, Mommy! Nobody's to move! The sitter lost her contact lens."

"We should get poor Daddy a drum. He just
tried to buy mine."

"Jeffy's throwin' up . . . my favorite doll!"

"Daddy, your sideburns are nice and neat, but your backburn is getting long."

"Then Dick said, 'Oh, look at Jane! Wow! That's for me!'"

"Let's sit in the back near the candy counter."

"They must sleep a lot in Heaven, 'cause every time I see pictures of angels, they're wearin' nightgowns."

"I don't think this is recommended for mature audiences."

"Oooh, yes! We'll take one of the gray ones and a black one."

"I think I'll freshen up a bit before dinner."

"I'm not finished reading it yet."

"It's all right now — your nose stopped bleeding."

"Maybe I ran out of blood."

"Daddy, does 'zillion' come after 'trillion'?"

"Billy! Walk! Don't run!"

"I'm just bein' O. J. Simpson."

"Why doesn't Daddy stay home for MY birthday like he did on George Washington's?"

"The best part 'bout Grandma being here for
lunch is we can sit 'boy, girl, boy, girl' . . ."

"Mommy, did you use to be sexy?"

"Daddy can do 22 grunts."

"Now, put the thread through the eye of the needle."

"I can't do it. The needle's squinting."

"Can somebody come get in bed with me? I feel all-alonely."

"Do I hafta do my homework?"

"I WAS a gentleman! I let her hit me first!"

"These doubledeck numbers are called
fractions."

"You better watch out, you better not cry, you better not pout, I'm tellin' you why —the Easter Bunny's comin' to town . . ."

"These colored ones are only chicken eggs.
REAL Easter eggs are the candy kind."

"Mommy, I don't have any more black jelly
beans. Did the Easter Bunny leave
any extras?"

"I think it's just a mild case of unfinished homework."

"Where was his guardian angel?"

"Let's take a commercial break."

"It's too warm for a sweater. March must be turnin' into a lamb."

"Washin' my marbles. Why?"

"Mommy's letting the plants out."

"Do we HAFTA say grace just for stew?"

"Can we do some exercises along with you, Daddy?"

"This can burn things when the sun is out.
That's why it's called a magnifrying glass."

"Can I try your skateboard, Mister?"

"I bet her kids hear her when she calls them."

"Does Mommy know you're using her shower cap?"

"God makes daddies tall so we can get things from the top shelf."

"Jeffy just totaled his tricycle."

"Can't we do like you do at grownup parties
— girls in the livin' room and guys
in the kitchen?"

"Did you know picture windows cost $800?
That's what Mr. Ferrell says his will cost."

"We better start bein' good 'cause if we
don't, I think Mommy might resign."

"That was a long time ago when Mommy was
still hidin' PJ under her dress."

"Who gift-wrapped your finger, Daddy?"

"... and be a good boy."
"Aw, Mommy! I wanna have fun."

"Did we leave a wake-up call for 7 o'clock?"

"How do you know Reggie Jackson brushes his teeth every morning?"

"I'm glad God thought up rainbows."

"Dinner will be ready as soon as we've fed the
cat and dogs, the turtle, goldfish, bird,
the hamsters. . . ."

"I think I'll go on a low broccoli diet."

"Have you decided where he'll go to college?"
"No, we're waiting to see how he'll do
in nursery school."

"Why are you throwing those books
into the trash?"

"We should be very kind to cats and dogs
because they have no words."

"I'm goin' to the bathroom, Jeffy.
Cover for me."

"Does pork come from porcupines?"

"When you put a quarter in you win an hour."

"We were on radar and we got blipped."

"Mommy, Billy's pulling 'May Fool' tricks
because it's May 1. Are we allowed
to do that?"

"But Daddy has HIS elbows on the table."

"That's a period. It means stop and take a breath."

"But how do you KNOW the light goes out in there whenever you shut the door?"

"Do I say 'Happy Mother's Day' on Grandma's or 'Happy Grandmother's Day'?"

"If they had Mother's Day on Monday, you
wouldn't have to do all this laundry."

"Mommy! PJ talked to a stranger! Do you want to scold him or shall I do it?"

"Our driveway has some cracks in it. Can we
get it repaved?"

"I'm waitin' for my flowers to come up."

"Can we stop to buy some crayons on the way home, Mommy?"

"He's a real good actor. He makes you think
he LIKES kissing girls."

"This broom is just my age!"

"I can lick any bowl in this kitchen."

"Know why I smell so good? I put a dab of
peanut butter behind each ear."

"Good night, lamp; good night, TV set; good night, plants; good night, chair; good night, other chair . . ."

"PJ! You're a male chauvinist piglet!"

"Grandma says boys should stand up when a lady comes into the room."

"Daddy's mowing his whiskers."

"Do you want me to help or can you do my
homework yourself?"

"The outside's almost ready to be morning."

"She's five, has a pony tail and her name's Dolly. Please tell her to get out here this minute."

"How are we supposed to give 'Parental Guidance' unless we go to see the picture?"

"This is handwriting. See, my name is all one piece."

"Daddy's wearing his talkin' ear muffs."

"Grandma always cuts it again so I can have
FOUR little sandwiches."

"Mommy, PJ won't come out of the closet to play with me."

"I know it's Saturday 'cause you have those
little stems all over your face."

"Daddy, when are we goin' over to the confession stand?"

"Vines like to shinny up poles."

"You just line up the arrow with the slot."

"Girls are called the opposite sex 'cause they always want to do the opposite of what we want to do."

"Mommy, come and see our dune!"

"Airplanes make roads in the sky out of smoke."

"At last, Mommy! The car's nice and clean!"

"On Father's Day we're gonna play with Daddy ALL DAY!"

"We made a card for Daddy. It says, 'To our
father who art in bed. . .'"

"Mommy, will you make me a sheet of cheese?"

"PJ's practicin' graffiti again!"

"I'm just pretendin' I'm an auto maker and I'm recalling this car."

"Mommy! My shoe swallowed up my sock!"

"Kids' voices were never so penetrating when I was little."

"Is it an ad for something, Daddy?"

"Enjoy them every minute, Deary. Before you can turn around they'll be grown."